By Vernice Walker, M. Ed.

Illustrated by TullipStudio

For My Dad & Past & Present Members of
The New Hope Rodeo & Community

Story Based on True Events

RODEO

"R, O, D, E, O, pronounce and tell us the meaning of this word," asked my 4th grade teacher,

Mr. Bradford. Mr. Bradford was my first male teacher and I think most of the girls in our classroom and I had a crush on him.

"R, O, D, E, O, I had no idea what the word meant or how it was pronounced. I had never seen the word before However, whatever came out of my mouth was something my classmates thought was very funny. I was embarrassed. Instead of guessing, I should have just said, I don't know."

Faith & Hope was the name of the community where Gramps and Grandma lived. I often got Faith & Hope confused with Summit, because the residents used the names interchangeably. Was Faith & Hope a town or community?

Each Friday evening or Saturday morning Momma would pack our bags and we'd travel to Gramps' and Grandma's house. A 4-door sedan was Dad's car of choice. It would be loaded down.

05

We stayed the weekends at our grandparents until one day
Dad and Mom had a house moved to the land of our own.

06

Gramps was a farmer.
When we'd visit, my siblings and
I would help with planting, weeding,
and harvesting his crop.

Gramps' crop consisted of
the sweetest cantaloupe,
watermelons of all sizes,

purple hull peas, onions with long green stems, corn on the cob, ruby red tomatoes, and okra. You name it; he grew it.
There was also a scarecrow on the fence post that scared more than the crows. It scared me, too!
08

These were long, hot summer days. It felt like we were working during the time the sun was at its peak. We'd have fresh lemonade to drink after completing our work, thanks to Grandma.

Dad was a busy man. He managed several restaurants in town.

So when he was busy, we kids knew not to bother him.

He was always working on something important. At the time, he was drawing something on a large piece of paper using rulers of all shapes and sizes.

10

FAITH & HOPE
RODEO

Once we arrived at the farm, we kids would work with Gramps in
the garden while Dad and his friends were building something.
I wasn't sure what. He was using the sheet he'd drawn using the
different shaped rulers. We would later learn Dad was building
his own rodeo grounds.

Most rodeos had a club of horseback riders, and each club had a queen that represented the riding club.

The clubs would travel from town to town, mostly on the weekends. They'd ride horses downtown, parade style. Each club would have matching satin jackets with their club names and symbols embossed on the back.

13

Club members rode quarter horses to Tennessee Walkers.
We'd see horses in all shades from ivory to charcoal black,
even pinto horses, too. It was cool to watch.

14

15

For fun Dad and Mom would take us to see events at other rodeos nearby. We had family and friends who competed in events like calf roping, bulldogging, and bull riding. We'd travel to Boley, OK; Clearview, OK; and Tullahassee, OK; just to name a few.

17

After our Dad finished putting the final touches on his rodeo grounds,
he was ready to make "Faith & Hope Round Up Club" known and he needed
a queen. There were several young ladies in the community that rode and
cared for their horses, but for some reason he chose me to represent our
club.

Why he chose me, I'll never know. A 10-year-old rodeo queen? I rode small
or medium sized horses that were tamed. This riding was done with
my cousins on our farm and not inside an arena with onlookers.

To know my Dad, some may describe him as determined, focused especially
during rodeo season. He was not one to take 'no' for an answer easily.

"Oh, it will be fun," he said. All I could think of was what if someone from
my school or neighborhood saw me in some sparkly get-up, I would be teased to
no end! I wasn't convinced it would be fun, either.

Daddy could be persuasive, even downright demanding, when he wanted to be.
I wouldn't be easily convinced, either. He and Momma went out and bought me
a lime-green polyester pant suit and matching hat. I still wasn't convinced.

FAITH & HOPE
RODEO
19

I was acquainted with some of the 'Queens' from the other roundup clubs. They did everything but sleep (Some may have!) with their horses.

I wasn't that attached. You've got to be kidding, I thought. "Daddy, I never said I agreed to this!" "Wait, wait a minute — hold on now. We have plenty of time to practice before the next parade," he said. We had several weeks to practice before the big event.

Each Saturday after finishing our chores, word spread to the "Naysayers" that I would be practicing in the empty arena. The Naysayers consisted of cousins, sisters and other non— horse— riding potential rodeo royalty, who was not chosen to represent the FHRC (Faith & Hope Rodeo Club).

In the arena enters Dad with a horse saddled and bridled for me to ride. I looked at the horse and then at Dad. "Oh, no you don't; I'm not riding that wild untamed horse!"
22

23

Of all the horses we had, he chose the wildest one of the bunch!
"This is the best—looking horse we have,"Dad said. I'd witnessed this
horse buck off numerous riders. In fact, Dad used him in the practice
rodeo as a bucking broncho! I was not an experienced rider, to put
it mildly, and no lime—green polyester pantsuit was going to make me
think otherwise.

Mom was in full agreement with him. which surprised me.
"Momma, I'd ride the one—eyed mare before riding that wild horse,"
I said; but Dad had convinced her, too.

The event date was inching near, and I hadn't mounted the horse, yet. Daddy grew worried. Would he have a rodeo queen or not? He had to think of a plan, so he decided to ride the horse and tire him down before handing the reigns over to me.

He took off down one side of the arena kicking up a cloud of dust and dirt. He made a couple of circles around the arena; when he stopped, Dad appeared almost as tired and sweaty as the horse. I still wasn't ready.

27

As R—day (Rodeo Day) approached, Dad came up with what would be his last and final idea. He enlisted the help of one of my older more experienced horse—riding cousins, Kevin, to ride on the same horse behind me. I trusted Kevin at this point more so than I trusted Dad. With him behind me, I felt safe from being bucked off or bitten by the horse.

I rode the horse full speed with Kevin behind me, kicking up dust and dirt of my own. I wasn't afraid, no worries at all. I looked over at the Naysayers. They seemed a bit disappointed. They were expecting to see something side-cracking worthy. There was not a bite or buck off with my riding partner Kevin behind me.

WATER

The date had finally arrived. I had sweated through my polyester pantsuit and Dad had done the same with his crisply starched white shirt. With the combined heat and humidity, it had to be over 100° with no wind at all.

33

Daddy decided we'd skip the parade downtown, which was fine by me. The parade of clubs was next. This event took place inside the arena. I thought, "If I fall, it would not hurt as much. The tilled dirt was soft and deep." After the state and national flags rode in, it was time for the Grand Entry. I was as nervous as a cat at a dog kennel convention. I knew my cousin Kevin was still riding behind me. This gave me the same sense of security, the same as I had back home.

And now, said the Rodeo Announcer (loud over the microphone so everyone could hear him) representing the Faith & Hope Rodeo Club, "I heard my name!" The horse took off from the entry gate like lightning. I held onto my hat as tight as the reigns. I lined my pony up right next to the former queen who was previously announced but for some reason my saddle felt lighter.

35

I felt behind me for my cousin Kevin, but I didn't feel anything. I looked around for him. I look towards the entry gate and there he was squatting down pointing his finger at me laughing as if to say, "You didn't need me after all; you had it all along."

37

I couldn't believe it! I rode the horse in on my own! Instead of Kevin riding behind me as we had practiced, my cousin hopped off the back of the horse during the announcement and yelled, "RUN!" I did it! I couldn't believe it! I rode the wild horse on my own full speed with out falling or being bucked off.

I looked throughout the stands at the throngs of people sitting in the bleachers. I was looking for the Naysayers. I couldn't find one of them anywhere.

39

But I could see Daddy.
He was standing by
the barbed wire fence
with a grin from ear to ear.